# CONTENTS:

Skye Bridge: a Personal View     7

The Good old Days!     11

**Mainland illustrations:**

*Cluanie to Glenelg*     17

*Letterfearn to Balmacara*     21

*Kyle of Lochalsh*     28

A Century of Motoring     53

**Skye illustrations:**

*Kyleakin to Sligachan with diversions*     64

*Portree to Uig via Staffin and Flodigarry*     78

*Skeabost to Dunvegan with diversions*     90

*The road to Armadale Pier*     96

ALL WORK

STOPS FOR

MACPHERSON'S

VEST POCKET

GUIDE

From 1927 until the 1950s, Duncan Macpherson published an annual guide for the convenience of travellers visiting Skye and Lochalsh. What better way for a photographer and postcard-publisher to advertise its availability!

# OVER TO SKYE...
# BEFORE THE BRIDGE!

## Nostalgic Album Views

## BOB CHARNLEY

Clan Books
Doune

Published by:

**cb**     **CLAN BOOKS**
**The Cross, Doune**
**Perthshire FK16 6BE**
**Tel: 01786 841330**
**Fax: 01786 841326**

First published 1995

ISBN: 1 873597 03 7

Printed by:

**Adlard Print & Typesetting Services**
**The Old School**
**The Green**
**Ruddington**
**Notts NG11 6HH**

# DEDICATION

What Dr Francis Smart did in Glenelg in 1889, and Procurator-Fiscal Archie Chisholm did in North Uist in the 1890s, **Duncan Macpherson, M.P.S., F.S.A. Scot.,** did in Kyle of Lochalsh for more than fifty years: he photographed everything!

Like his fellow enthusiasts, Duncan used his camera to record much of what was happening around him from the years just prior to World War I through to the early 1960s. Scenery, local personalities, dwellings large or humble, opening ceremonies, street collections, people at work and play; ships calling at Kyle bound for Glasgow, Portree or the Outer Isles – all were dutifully captured on glass or celluloid, and copies sold to the public either as postcards, or as enlargements to be carried off, framed and hung on the walls of distant homes.

Born in Glenquithel in Aberdeen-shire, Duncan moved to Kyle in 1911, *"...a tall, miserably thin young man setting foot on the rocky West in search of a livelihood..."* He married, raised a family and remained in Kyle, dispensing the necessities of life from the premises of what he called his *'modest pharmacy'*. Over the next five decades, Macpherson found time to write books, provide articles and photographs for distant newspapers and sit on the local council, but it was his skill with the camera that elevated his *'Kyle Pharmacy Series'* postcards of Skye and Lochalsh above those produced by Valentine's of Dundee, Raphael Tuck, Judges of Hastings and many other publishers. He did, however, have some enormous advantages over his rivals: his shop and dark-room were in the centre of the village, he lived locally and he knew everyone. He was always readily available to record local events and happenings, and consequently his surviving pictures and negative collection are an important record of an age that has now almost vanished completely.

Macpherson's photographs greatly influenced the style of my own image collection while it was being formed, and with the permission of his daughter Mary – who has generously loaned some of her father's rarer images of Kyle – I am proud to be able to dedicate this book to the life and times of Duncan Macpherson (1882-1966) *master-photographer.*

A balmy day in Kyle of Lochalsh and a picture for 'nostalgia' buffs of the future: the *Loch Fyne* in 1995, her final year on the Kyle-Kyleakin route.

## SKYE BRIDGE: A PERSONAL VIEW

**I**N THE YEAR 2005, today's Kyleakin teenagers will be telling their own children about those times when a car-ferry ran between Kyle and Skye. Nostalgia – supposedly something only those over the age of forty indulged in — will come early to the next generation of Kyleakin parents as they recall their own childhood experiences aboard the ferry while travelling to school or shadowing mother on her week-end shopping trip to Kyle. At the end of 1995, Skye-bound travellers will have to drive over a bridge while humming the tune of that famous *"Speed, bonnie boat ..."* ditty, yet despite the presence of this latest monument to progress, car-ferries from Mallaig and Glenelg will still carry the romancers of this world *"...over the sea to Skye"* so all will not be lost!

The panorama of Kyle and Kyleakin before the Skye Bridge: a 1930s sepia postcard published by Judges of Hastings who still produce postcards today from their premises in St. Leonards-on-Sea, East Sussex.

Strange that it took so long to bridge the gap at Kyle. Should it not have been done thirty years ago when summer-time traffic blocked Kyle and Kyleakin for hours on end? A feasibility study in the 1960s had already concluded that a bridge could be built within the space of three years at a cost of just under £3,000,000 but someone in Inverness had other ideas and the ferry service was upgraded instead. With the advantage of hindsight that was probably a blunder although some might disagree:

*"Why on earth do we need a bridge to Skye...It will only attract more cars and visitors. And what about damage to the environment...It's fragile enough as it is."*

If that was the gist of your argument then the new Skye Bridge will be a big disappointment. Doubtless, should a calamity strike the island in the near future, the bridge will get all the blame.

About seven centuries ago – and some of this might just be a bit of a fairy story – a Norwegian princess lived in Kyleakin at *Caisteal Maol,* that ruin of a castle which, like some loutish football fan questioning a referee's parentage, appears to be gesturing rudely towards the mainland. Bored with the monotony of her daily routine, and supposedly short of a few of the adornments that princesses like to have about their person, the girl came up with a little scheme that would occupy her time and supplement the meagre allowance she received from her husband, variously described as either a follower of Clan MacDonald or of Mackinnon of Strath – but who cares about him anyway, his wife is the real star! Legend has it she placed an iron ring into rocks at Kyle, affixed a strong chain, stretched it across the narrows, secured it to the Skye shore and waited. And when the first boat sailed down the water and ran into the chain she emerged from her castle.

*"Pay up and then you may pass,"* she demanded, and pay they did! For that trick with the chain – one assumes it was for that and not for some other nasty little habit – the princess earned herself the nickname 'Saucy Mary', and certain people have suggested that this name be given to the new bridge! But 'Saucy Mary' or not, the bridge has been built with an eye to the future, when, before too long, dusky individuals from the southern regions of the federated European Union will desert their olive groves and goats and head north, intent on grabbing a share of the wealth being generated by the petroleum companies working off Skye. Already the bridge is looking too small; it will surely have to be widened if it is to cope with the traffic of the next century!

Twentieth century Royalty at Kyleakin. The Duke and Duchess of York (H.M. The Queen Mother) in September 1933, with the 16th century ruin of *Caisteal Maol* in the background, the supposed site of 'Saucy Mary's' home. A postcard published by Kyle pharmacist Duncan Macpherson.

While it was being built, the bridge suffered from a brief headline-grabbing period of siege. The itinerant professional protesters eventually left Kyle – some undoubtedly made career moves, headed for England and ended up in trees next to the M11 extension or chained to earth-moving machines at Twyford Down – but the Scottish press continued to publish letters from equally indignant but more peaceful critics. Protest campaigns were orchestrated by exiles – 'Scots' living in those warm countries to which their ancestors had been transported on the orders of their own clan chiefs over a century ago – and a letter from a resident of New South Wales may have reflected the thoughts of many others:

*"...business people, hoteliers...and various non-descript politicians with only pound signs in their eyes thought it [the bridge] would bring them added business. They didn't think, or care, that it would also take business away. The bridge will not only be unsightly and expensive but unsafe."*

Some nomad probably said much the same thing when he saw the Great Pyramid being built at Giza; what an eyesore that must have appeared to be at that time!

A few people (while actually campaigning for *other* causes) accused the 'London' Government of building *"an unwanted toll-bridge..."* and of agreeing to a *"sub-standard"* box girder type *"...funded by the Bank of America."* Others insisted that since foot-passengers had been carried free of charge on the old ferry (a *remarkably* generous and recent concession by Caledonian MacBrayne, not granted to users on any of their other routes) local buses should offer the same service to their passengers. One campaigner contrived to link these matters to the effects of local unemployment, the disadvantages of bypassing Kyleakin and the destruction of Scots Pines behind the Lochalsh Hotel; her letter ended with a request that contributions *"towards the fight against the unwanted toll-bridge..."* be sent to a numbered building society account – set up for the salvation of *"the Otters of Scotland"*! Fortunately, thanks to the joint partnership of bridge builders Miller-Dywidag, Scots Pine seedlings have been planted on the mainland side, and the otters below the bridge will probably be the most pampered and protected group in the whole of Scotland. The company spent hundreds of thousands of pounds providing them with new holts, freshwater pools and a network of tunnels.

Certainly the bridge caused controversy and the arguments were fierce to the point of acrimony, but debates tend to drag on and have to be cut short if progress is to be made. The Skye Bridge is now a reality, and while some may shake their fists at it in anger, travellers from distant lands stood and gasped in amazement in 1995, previously unaware of its existence because of what might be described as a little local 'attitude problem' on Skye.

Three official publications were available at the beginning of the year: Caledonian MacBrayne's 'Day Sails' leaflet for Mallaig, Kyle and Skye; the Automobile Association's first 'Road Information Update' leaflet, and the guide of the Skye and South-West Ross Tourist Board.

*"Please be advised that this* [Kyle] *service will be withdrawn on the opening of the Skye Bridge ..."* reported CalMac. The AA also forewarned their members, giving six months notice of the proposed opening, but the official Skye Tourist Guide was less forthcoming in its introduction:

*"Millions of years ago Skye and South-West Ross were joined. Today only a narrow channel, formed by glaciation, separates them. So it's natural to look at the two together...Driving to Skye, you can enjoy the magnificent mountains, lochs and historic attractions of South-West Ross before taking the Kyle of Lochalsh-Kyleakin ferry or the Glenelg-Kylerhea ferry..."*

A geological explanation for the watery gap but no word about the bridge. No mention, either, in the 'Events 1995' section on page twenty, yet here was a bridge that was being built to *replace* the ferry at the most important access point for visitors. With completion less than eight months away, some of the 'ostriches' up in Portree still had their heads firmly buried in the sand as far as the bridge was concerned. Having rejected impartiality for their own brand of politics, perhaps those same officials will stick to their principles and in future only cross to the mainland on the Kylerhea or Armadale ferry!

As the last few years of the 20th century slipped away, and the possibility of a bridge to Skye was debated once more, Caledonian MacBrayne built bigger ships and switched to a 24 hour service on the Kyle-Kyleakin route, but it was all too late! In April 1991, Miller-Dywidag's submission for the fixed crossing was accepted by the Secretary of State for Scotland; perhaps if *Loch Dunvegan* and *Loch Fyne* had been built a decade sooner they, or their successors, could have been ferrying vehicles from Kyle to Kyleakin in the year 2000.

Many will mourn the passing of the Kyle ferry. For visitors it was an enjoyable part of an annual holiday, although it could be a bit of a chore for regular users when the roads were crowded and the ferry queues long. Nevertheless, it was a major link with the mainland and its presence brought about great improvements to the roads on Skye, especially between Kyleakin and the ferry terminal at Uig. But over distances as short as this, it surely makes sense to replace all ferries by tunnels, bridges or causeways. The lovelorn bachelors on the island of Vatersay discovered that for themselves a few years ago when their passenger-only ferry was replaced by a causeway from Barra. Lucky lads, now they can travel backwards and forwards every hour of the day, but for them the crossing is entirely *toll-free!*

*Bob Charnley*
*June 1995*

# THE GOOD OLD DAYS!

**W**HEN THE Skye Bridge was half-built the press reported that 80 per cent of the island's population did not want it, but in truth (especially after having heard what the proposed toll might be) none of the islanders wanted to have to pay to use it. Nearly sixty years ago, in 1939, Duncan Macpherson F.S.A. Scot., renowned photographer, author and proprietor of *The Kyle Pharmacy*, expressed similar concern when the car-ferry at Dornie was about to be replaced by a toll-bridge:

*"Lochalsh stands alone. It is unique. Separated by mountain and sea from the rest of Scotland, it is the only parish to which there is no access. True, a bridge is being built across Loch Long to connect it with Kintail and the south. Probably due to a movement for the revival of ancient customs, motorists will have to pay a toll. It may be anticipated that the public will flock to the Highlands to see this anachronism – a British toll-bridge on a public highway, built A.D. 1940!"*

Dornie ferry in 1935. *"The ferry across Loch Long need not cause fear to any motorist,"* wrote Iain F. Anderson in 1934 in his book 'The Sunset Shore'. *"To embark one's car you run down a very rough jetty and make a half-turn to the right to bounce on to the ferry turntable. It is a movement that requires caution...but it need not cause fear even to the novice, if he keeps to low gear and obeys the instructions of the ferryman ..."* Anderson was driving 'Snippy', his 1932 8 h.p. Morris Minor saloon.

In its last full year of operation the Dornie ferry ran continuously from 8 a.m. to 8 p.m., Sundays and Bank Holidays included, although travellers could expect to be delayed for up to two hours at low tide. Crossings after 8 p.m. were at the discretion of the ferry master but after 10 p.m. the normal charge of 6/- (30p) for car and driver was raised by fifty per cent. *For non-Britons – and Britons who cannot remember the 'good old days' prior to decimalisation! – 12 pennies (d) made one shilling (1/-) and 20/- made £1.* That same year (1939) the ferry at Ballachulish cost 2/6d – 5/- for cars over

16 horse-power – and 6/- at Kylesku. When bridges replaced these ferries (Dornie in 1940, Ballachulish in 1975 and Kylesku in 1984) only at Dornie was a toll ever levied. It lasted for six years, until the end of World War II, and was discontinued on the grounds that the bridge had become an integral part of the national highway system.

The car ferry at Ballachulish in 1926. In 1988, a suitcase containing a collection of private motoring photographs and original negatives was discovered on a stall in an antiques market in Bath. All the pictures were taken in Scotland in 1925 and 1926, and this picture is now sold in and around Ballachulish as a sepia postcard.

A 1913 receipt from Ballachulish ferryman Alex McNab for two weeks' wages – £3.00.

But if, in the guise of Lochalsh Parish Councillor, Duncan Macpherson had had his way in the 1930s, the bridge across Loch Long would never have been built in the first place. He tells the story in chapter 22 – The Road to Nowhere – of 'Gateway to Skye', a delightful book written in 1939 but not published until 1946. The chapter opens:

*"It was unfortunate for the parish of Lochalsh that Caesar did not find the opportunity to reach it. That great road-maker would not have left it in its present state of isolation. Its unique position is a source of wonder to many who do not know Highland conditions. Before motor cars came into common use, the roads and footpaths which served for internal communication throughout the parish were probably sufficient. Many places were more readily accessible by sea than by road, for three sides of Lochalsh are surrounded by sea..."*

In essence, the residents of Kyle and all who travelled from Skye using the Kyleakin crossing were trapped by two ferries: Dornie and Strome. Freedom to progress beyond these places could be restricted by low tides, bad weather, lengthy queues, occasional motor-boat failure or, as at Strome, the Sabbath, but a solution was possible if politicians and the officers of Ross-shire and Inverness-shire County Councils were prepared to listen. The key to the whole matter involved the road at Nostie running *via* Conchra and Sallachy to Killilan alongside Loch Long. If it was improved, together with the private track running from Killilan to Benula Lodge through Glen Elchaig, a new stretch of road could then be constructed to meet up with what is now the A831 at Cannich. As a consequence, the route to Inverness would be 12 miles shorter and both ferries avoided. The idea had originally been proposed by George Mackay, a dissenting member of a Government committee set up in 1918 to study the future of rural transport in Scotland, but his fellow members favoured the railway system and had little time for roads in the north of Scotland:

*"To fit the roads for heavy traffic would probably entail an initial outlay of about £2,000 per mile and the maintenance charges would also be heavy. The making of improved roads would cost nearly as much as the construction of a narrow gauge light railway."*

Duncan Macpherson was full of enthusiasm for Mackay's road – he unashamedly drew attention to its potential in his 1923 book of photogravure illustrations titled 'Isles and Peaks of the West' – and when chosen to represent Lochalsh on the District Committee of the County Council he immediately tabled a motion for its construction; unfortunately, a motion for the building of a bridge across Loch Long came up at the very same council meeting! Macpherson was only prepared to accept the *status quo* as far as Dornie ferry was concerned and insisted on the new road. The people in Glenshiel, however, were stuck on the *other* side of the loch and a journey to Lochalsh, Strome or the new road to Inverness would still involve them in a ferry crossing. Their representative Colin Campbell stood up at the meeting and argued his case while Macpherson listened and made notes:

*"The principal spokesman in favour of the bridge scheme quoted figures to shew that one sheep and, approximately, the forequarters of another crossed Dornie ferry every three hours. In moving terms he pictured the plight of these innocent sheep being held up owing to bad weather. So realistic were his words that I could almost visualise the hind legs of some unfortunate animal shivering there on the cold, wet pier. But in case there were any in that meeting too hard-hearted*

*to consider the woes of the sheep, he used a further and more convincing argument. He pointed out that not only did the sheep suffer hardship, but that the delay affected their price at the sales!"*

The vote went against Macpherson and in favour of what he deemed to be *"the fantastic proposal"* of a bridge at Dornie. He may have lost the battle but he went down fighting:

*"The bridge will link up the parishes of Lochalsh and Kintail, and will enable the inhabitants of those districts to meet more easily at social functions. Certainly, for local traffic, it will be most useful; and as a fake museum-piece it will doubtless attract the attention of antiquarians. But as part of a National road, or even a through road to Skye, it will be an absurdity."*

Despite his initial opposition to the bridge, Macpherson quickly accepted it and in later editions of his annual 'Pocket Guide to Skye and Lochalsh' he called it a *"fine ferro-concrete bridge spanning Loch Long."*

From the shore below Robin's Nest restaurant and Dornie village hall in 1990, one could observe the final stages of construction of the present bridge; months later, heavy machines arrived and attacked its predecessor. That 1940 'absurdity' may have been frail and thin but it had served the public for over 50 years and it died a horrible lingering death, its decaying supports still pointing threateningly skyward long after the spans had been removed.

The 1940 'absurdity' that replaced the ferry across Loch Long at Dornie – Dornie Bridge in the 1950s.

At the beginning of this century the charge for transporting a car between Kyle and Kyleakin was 10/- (50p), not that there were many takers. The ferry was nothing more than a small rowing boat, and the roads on Skye were so poor that few motorists were willing to risk their expensive tyres on them. Those who were prepared to venture onto the ferry were covered against the loss of their car by an insurance policy taken out by the Highland Railway Company, holders of the ferry rights. Twenty years later the price was still the same, but now the car was balanced on two planks tied across a slightly larger rowing boat than before, and either rowed to Kyleakin or towed behind a motor launch. From the outset the service was run by private contractors, local men appointed by the railway company because of their knowledge of the waters, but in 1935 MacBrayne's took over the lease and a two-car vessel eventually replaced the old mode of transport. By 1939 the charge for a small car had dropped to 8/- (40p); by 1995 it had reached £5.40, or £3.10 for holders of a pre-paid book of 10 tickets, but the total number of vehicles using the ferry each year was never publicly revealed. Based, however, on figures given to Miller-Dywidag by the Scottish Office, approximately 402,500 cars, 31,000 commercial vehicles and 6,500 coaches would have been ferried to and from Skye during 1994.

Back in 1939, when the Kyle ferry operated during daylight hours only, the motorist who missed the last sailing could console himself over dinner at the Lochalsh Hotel and then retire for the night. The next morning, after enjoying a substantial breakfast, he would receive a bill for sixteen shillings (80p), twice the price of his ticket for the ferry crossing. With a 24-hour ferry service operating in the 1990s the traveller was inconvenienced no more, and the necessity to spend £87.50 (the 1995 price for a single room with dinner and breakfast at the Lochalsh Hotel) had gone. The inescapable conclusion, therefore, is that Caledonian MacBrayne were undercharging by about £38 a car in 1995 *or* dinner, bed and breakfast at the hotel should have been £10.80 a night. Wishful thinking of course – CalMac and the hotel guests would have been the only ones rejoicing – but try the same trick with something less luxurious from the thirties such as a gallon of petrol, a bottle of whisky or a wickedly-dangerous packet of 20 Player's Navy Cut cigarettes which cost a ha'penny under 1/- in 1939; a pack now costs *sixty* times its pre-war amount whereas the final ferry price was only thirteen and a half times higher. As to the price for dinner and a night of comfort and luxury at the Lochalsh Hotel, the management *might* be prepared to 'do a deal' if things are that quiet, but the attendant in the toll-booth will offer no such discounts at 2 o'clock in the morning!

The illustrations that now follow are a celebration of the 'good old days' – years before a Skye Bridge was ever dreamt of – and the emphasis is very much on the mode of travel between the years 1900 and 1939.

From the old inn at Cluanie we will travel down to Glenelg and visit the site of the original ferry between mainland and Skye; then to Letterfearn and across Loch Long to Dornie. Crossing over to Ardelve and passing through Balmacara we stop off in Kyle of Lochalsh to see the sights and indulge in some ship-watching! A ferry will then take us across to Kyleakin for a short trip around Skye before we travel down to Armadale for the return journey to the mainland. This will be a brief tour of Skye: time (space in this case) never allows the day-tripper to see everything anyway!

Good old days? Judge that for yourself as you look at the pictures and read the random musings, but while wiping away your tears as you view roads devoid of cars or seas full of beautiful swift steamers, just remember the words of traveller, author and naval captain Frederick Marryat (1792-1848):

*"Those who are solely governed by the past, stand, like Lot's wife, crystallized in the act of looking backward, and for ever incapable of looking forward."*

*SCOTLAND'S WONDERLAND*

# THE ROYAL ROUTE
to
# THE WESTERN HIGHLANDS

and

## ISLANDS OF SCOTLAND

### TOURIST PROGRAMME
### AND TIME TABLE
(MAY to SEPTEMBER)

of the Royal Mail Steamers of

## DAVID MACBRAYNE LIMITED
119 HOPE STREET　　　　　GLASGOW, C. 2

**1928**

*Printed in Great Britain*

# CLUANIE TO SKYE *VIA* GLENELG

1.      Our journey starts at **Cluanie Inn** just before the outbreak of World War I: an isolated spot on a lonely stretch of road but a welcome halt for the driver of the Wigan-registered (EK 457) automobile. Near here, sheep and deer may reduce the speed of today's motorist but be prepared for trouble! Three miles further on, devil-like creatures inhabit the dark forest of the glen (seriously, they *do!*) and they occasionally wander into the road and startle the unwary.

2.      **Glenshiel Post Office** – now just a memory – and a group of Edwardian tourists who look like they have just come straight off their cruise ship. *"Visited this place, July 23rd 1913. Cloudless sky,"* is the brief comment on the reverse of this postcard.

GLEN SHIEL FILLING STATION, LOCH DUICH

**3.**     The road to Skye: **Glen Shiel Filling Station** as it was in the early 1960s when the route of the main road went to the *left* of the garage and took all Kyle-bound drivers over Shiel Bridge itself.

LOCH DUICH FROM THE SUMMIT OF MAMRATAGAN, NEAR GLENELG, INVERNESS-SHIRE.            8197.

**4.**     View from the summit of **Mam Ratagan** in the 1930s. Trees *had* been planted – with a strong magnifying glass they can just be seen on the original photograph – but many expressed opposition at the time and one writer warned: *"With such masses of fir trees...they may tend to screen the view from the road as they grow up. If that happens it will be well to leave the car at the top for the engine to cool down and take a stroll along the hills on the right ..."* (Arthur Gardner, **'Western Highlands'** 1947).

**5.** *"The trees about the Old Manse were to me like people. With each visit, they and I seemed to get to know one another intimately…after the companionship of bird and beast – and for me, at any rate, the sea – give me the companionship of a tall cluster of trees growing close to a dwelling-place."* The thoughts of author Alasdair Alpin MacGregor following a visit to the manse in the 1930s. Within the walled-garden there is now a visitors' centre which houses the workshop of 'Glenelg Candles', a coffee-shop (with wonderfully *wicked* rich cakes!), and exhibition space where local paintings and enlargements of some rare Victorian photographs of Glenelg can be seen and purchased.

**6.** A little detour from the road to the Glenelg ferry will take the traveller to the main street of **Glenelg Village.** This card was produced by Ewen Cameron of Glenelg *circa* 1906 and the Post Office (on the left) is still operating from the same building today.

THE FERRY AT KYLERHEA.

A.4648

**7.** **Kylerhea** (Glenelg) **Ferry** in 1936 when it carried just one car. *Glenachulish*, the present ferry, can accommodate up to six vehicles and is commanded by the redoubtable Capt. Roddy MacLeod. It operates from Easter to late autumn. Travelling to or from Skye, visitors should make *at least* one trip on this ferry but for the best views try the crossing from Kylerhea to Glenelg.

## No. 7. GLENELG to KYLERHEA (SKYE).
### Across Sound of Sleat.

*Photograph by Duncan Macpherson, Kyle of Lochalsh.*

Motor Ferry Boat. Service commences 1st April and finishes 31st October. Continuous service, 8 a.m. to 9.30 p.m., from May to August inclusive, and from 9 a.m. till half an hour before dusk in April, September, and October. Delay of up to two hours at very low tides only. NO SUNDAY SERVICE.

|  | Single | Return |
|---|---|---|
| Motor-car, 12 h.p. and under | 8   0 | 14   0 |
| ,, ,, over 12 h.p. | 10   0 | 17   0 |
| Tri-cars | 6   0 | 10   6 |
| Motor-cycles (solo) | 2   6 | 4   0 |
| Motor-cycle and sidecar | 5   0 | 9   0 |
| Passengers | 0   6 | 0   9 |

Return tickets valid for 21 days.

**8.** From the Automobile Association's 1936 edition of **'Ferries in Scotland'**; details and prices for the Glenelg Ferry.

**9.**      At the head of **Loch Duich** with the Five Sisters as a backdrop. Our friend with the Wigan-registered car who was at Cluanie Inn earlier (*illus.* **1**) appears to have the road very much to himself!

**10.**      H.M. King Edward VII descending the specially-built Royal Pier at Letterfearn during his visit to Loch Duich on 21 September, 1904. *"He thought the Five Sisters the most wonderful he had seen,"* commented Duncan Macpherson in **'Gateway to Skye'.** *"In his day he had known many sisters. He could speak from experience!"*

**11.**    The ferryman's house at **Totaig**, *circa* 1910, departure point for the folk from Letterfearn crossing to Dornie or Ardelve. The driver of that Wigan-registered car beat us to it: he is parked at the end of the road! *"There's a bar attached to the little white house on the Totaig side of the ferry,"* wrote Alasdair Alpin MacGregor in 1935 in **'Somewhere in Scotland'**. *"West Highland ferries, as you may know, are frequently an excuse for bars!"*

Dornie Ferry, Loch Long

**12.**    The **Dornie Ferry** on Loch Long in the 1890s, and the ladies remained seated in the carriage while the driver calmed the horses during the crossing. This postcard, published by George Washington Wilson of Aberdeen *circa* 1905, was posted from Balmacara in August, 1910, and has a terse message, probably intended for the sender's house-keeper (Mrs Fletcher) at The Cottage, The Willows, Lytham, Lancashire: *"I have told Snape to come up to look at the pictures on the stairs on Monday. If he does not come, send for him..."*

**13.    Eilean Donan Castle:** an 1880s photograph on a postcard published by George Washington Wilson in Aberdeen *circa* 1905. Somewhat damaged by the English in 1719, the castle was rebuilt two hundred years later by Colonel MacRae-Gilstrap. Posted from Balmacara on 7 September, 1910, Mrs Fletcher at The Cottage in Lytham, is still receiving instructions: *"A parcel was sent this morning to you. Please wait and take to the house – not here – as we return next week."* The growth of the telephone network eventually put an end to the use of postcards for such purposes.

**14.**    A wet July day in 1932, but Duncan Macpherson was ready with his camera, attending the opening ceremony of the new Eilean Donan Castle – undoubtedly now in the top three for the title of 'The Most Photographed Castle in Scotland'. *"Few of the natives of Dornie went to bed that night,"* remarked Alasdair Alpin MacGregor, attending the opening in his capacity as correspondent for *The Times*. *"The occasion had attracted such large numbers of people from considerable distances that every house in the village was filled to overflowing..."*

The Funds For This Ambulance Were Collected From Clansmen, Clanswomen, and Friends, at Home and Abroad, by Mrs Mac Rae - Gilstrap of Eilean Donan, 1914-16.

**15.** The **'Clan MacRae' Ambulance** and the caption says it all: *"The funds for this ambulance were collected from clansmen, clanswomen and friends, at home and abroad, by Mrs MacRae-Gilstrap of Eilean Donan, 1914-16."*

Dornie Ferry, Loch Duich

**16.** The passenger-ferry at Dornie *circa* 1901. *"We reached Dornie Ferry, where, with one honourable exception (and he was an American) we found every man connected with the ferry hopelessly drunk, in honour of a cattle show. Some were surly; some were cheery; others helplessly imbecile ..."* (Mrs C. Gordon Cumming, **'In the Hebrides'** 1883).

At the Ferry, Dornie.

154.

**17.** Thirty years after the previous picture was taken, Duncan Macpherson stood at the same place to record the progress of JS 2340 as it waited to cross from Ardelve to Dornie. *"Care necessary on approach from the south – steep, winding hill,"* was the advice offered by the Automobile Association in 1939 to drivers heading towards the ferry from the other side. As you approach the bridge across Loch Long today, a road-sign should caution: *"Eilean Donan Castle ahead. Beware of pedestrians wandering in the road."*

542    Dornie Bridge Opening 30th April, 1940

**18.** The world was now at war – the German invasion of Norway and Denmark had taken place just three weeks before – but on Tuesday 30 April, 1940, the people of Lochalsh district gathered for a more pleasurable occasion: the opening ceremony for the **Dornie Bridge**. Only the presence of a toll-booth marred their celebrations!

25

The Village, Ardelve

**19.**    Across Loch Long now, and on the way to Kyle: a mixture of the old and the new greets the traveller passing through **Ardelve** in the last quarter of the 19th century.

THE VILLAGE, BALMACARA.    BCA. 3

Copyright Lilywhite (1932) Ltd.
Sowerby Bridge

**20.**    Village and general stores in **Balmacara** *circa* 1935.

**21.**     Launched in 1904 – and attacked by a U-boat in 1918 while on passage to Barra – the ***S.S. Plover*** was a true work-horse, carrying cargo and passengers from Oban to Kyle, the Outer Isles and small west coast villages such as Balmacara. She was eventually scrapped in 1951.

**22.**  Routes to Skye have changed considerably over the last sixty years. The coast road to Kyle of Lochalsh beyond Balmacara was only constructed in the 1970s. Previously, travellers turned to the right before Balmacara House and entered Kyle *via* the hamlet of **Erbusaig,** seen here on a postcard published by Duncan Macpherson *circa* 1913.

**23.**  A photograph **of Kyle of Lochalsh Station,** *circa* 1899, with *'Skye Bogie'* Class locomotive number 85 – built in 1892 for the Highland Railway Company to use on their route to Strome Ferry. The line was extended to Kyle of Lochalsh at a cost of £17,000 per mile and the first train arrived in 1897.

**24.**    The main street of Kyle prior to World War I, with *"…one side lined with bank, post-office and shops, the other with bank, hotel, and gardens. In the distance a heather-clad hill loomed up."* (**'Gateway to Skye'**).

**25.**    Kyle's **Lifeboat Day** in 1931. The collectors have 'got their man' – in this case Peter Anderson the local telegraph boy – but one young lady ignores the camera and turns away. She had seen it all before however: Daddy was taking the photograph!

**26.** Pipe Major Macleod and pipers of the Lewis Pipe Band – accompanied by the usual gaggle of small boys – head a small contingent of soldiers returning to Stornoway from their Territorial Army camp in 1935. Posting the card from Kyle in August, 1935, to her daughter in Heaton Mersey, Manchester, 'mother' complained: *"We were kept awake last night with a pipe band playing for a dance. They didn't break up until 4 o'clock…"*

**27.** It is now the early fifties; the Bank of Scotland has had a smart coat of paint applied to their building and the Lewis Pipe Band entertains the crowd and the occupants of the cars stuck in the queue for the ferry.

**28.**     With the road temporarily closed to traffic, two young boys watch intently as the steam roller does its duty outside the Kyle Hotel. A private photograph taken by Duncan Macpherson in the 1930s.

**29.**     Once upon a time…well, kippers from Kyle could have been as famous as those from the Isle of Man but it just did not work out that way. Naval buildings now stand on the site of Kyle's former **Kipper Factory,** seen here on a pre 1914 postcard.

**30.** **Kyle Pharmacy** in the 1930s. *"The shop of the M.P.S. is a kind of modern Rialto 'where merchants most do congregate'...One can purchase most things at this shop from a seidlitz powder to a motor boat. He will develop and print your photos within twenty-four hours, and is himself an expert photographer in all its branches... he will arrange for you a motor boat sail up Loch Duich...and will supply you with books to read on the way should you tire of the wonderland..."* (Thomas Nicol **'Through Bracken and Heather'** 1935). A few of Macpherson's landscape photographs decorate the left-hand window; the other has advertising posters and cut-outs provided by the Kodak salesman. Outside, a slot machine dispenses Kodak film in three popular sizes.

**31.** The premises of the present Kyle Pharmacy – Geoff Webster M.(Royal)P.S. – is located in the building on the left of this picture. The cars outside Macpherson's shop (sometime during the 1930s) were in the queue for the ferry.

**32.** It was hard work for the boatmen and it could be dangerous for the novice passenger: the reality of a crossing between Kyle and Kyleakin in the 1890s. The sender of this George Washington Wilson hand-coloured postcard made her crossing on Friday 7 September 1906 and posted the card in Kyleakin: *"We came over in a little boat less than the one in the photo ..."* Twenty years earlier, a traveller was startled by *"the scramble of young natives to secure a fair share of our luggage and coin ..."* at this ferry.

**33.** The first version of the Kyle-Kyleakin car-ferry prior to World War I: one car – plus occupants – and four oarsmen in a flat-bottomed boat.

Over the sea to Skye from Kyle.

**34.** The *improved* version of the car-ferry in the 1920s. The vehicle is now balanced on planks laid across the boat and towed behind a small motor boat which carries driver and passengers.

THE FERRY KYLE OF LOCHALSH

**35.** The Mark 3 version of the Kyle-Kyleakin car-ferry, *circa* 1931, equipped with turntable and ramps but still only capable of carrying one vehicle. The Glenelg Motor launch is on the other side of the jetty. Her time-table varied with the seasons but she usually left Glenelg just before 9.00 a.m. (Monday to Saturday) for the seventy-five minute journey to Kyle, departing at 2.45 p.m. for the return trip. In July and August she would make an evening run from Glenelg arriving back by 8 o'clock.

**36.**     Far off days prior to World War I, and spectators watch as the crew of the rowing-boat prepare for the crossing to Kyleakin. Meanwhile, the man in the steam boat tinkers with the boiler ready for his own adventure on the calm waters of Loch Alsh. The 1900 edition of Black's **'Guide to Scotland'** mentioned that a steam ferry was already operating between Kyle and Kyleakin.

**37.**    A fine picture of 'travellers' in front of the gates of the Station (now Lochalsh) Hotel: a private photograph taken by Duncan Macpherson in the 1930s.

**38.**    The back of the ferry queue in the 1920s, and a family of 'travellers' pose at the side of the hairdresser's shop while Duncan Macpherson takes his picture.

**39.**    Just nine cars queuing for the Kyleakin ferry in the late 1920s, but the chances of the driver of the last car (a 1928 model Ford Tudor) being on Skye in anything under three hours were pretty slim!

**40.**     A Skye-bound caravan at Kyle in the 1930s...

**41.**     ...and the onlookers arrive to watch it being loaded onto the ferry. Caravan, car and driver were reunited on the next trip.

Ferrying a 'bus to Skye

**42.** A small bus being loaded onto the ferry in the 1930s. It may have been heading for Neil Beaton's garage in Portree, destined to spend its entire motoring-life on Skye.

265. "Over the Sea to Skye" from Kyle of Lochalsh

**43.** Kyle jetty in 1931. The Kyleakin-bound ferry has been loaded and heads off while the crowd of wet and wind-blown spectators watch the paddle steamer *Fusilier* 'smoke away' from the railway pier with the Royal Mail for Portree. The bow of the *Lochness* can be seen on the left of the picture.

**44.** The Glenelg Motor launch is at the jetty but the queue is for the Skye ferry. At least the rain was not falling on the crowd of more than 100 people waiting to make their crossing. A postcard published in the early 1930s.

**45.** First came *ML Kyle* (1916) then *Skye*, MV's *Kyleakin, Moil, Cuillin, Coruisk, Lochalsh,* and, in 1951, **Portree.** This private photograph was taken by Duncan Macpherson, probably on the very day *Portree* first arrived at Kyle: the paint-work is spotless – no rust spots visible – and the old tyres have yet to be hung over the sides!

KYLE OF LOCHALSH AND NEW FERRY BOAT, "PORTREE".          B.7835.

**46.** A new look, a new era and a new name: the former Station Hotel, having been much improved and enlarged, eventually emerged as **The Lochalsh Hotel.** A picture from the 1950s with *TSMV Portree* at the pier.

**47.**     In the final decade of the 20th century, with so much personally-owned transport available, it may be difficult to comprehend the importance to the local community of ships such as the **SS Claymore**. When this photograph was taken in 1912, MacBrayne's had some thirty-six vessels, *Mabel* the smallest at 30 tons and *Chieftain* – with a gross tonnage of 1080 – the largest; *Claymore,* launched July 1881, was number two in the fleet at 760 tons and operated between Glasgow and Stornoway. She carried every type of cargo – a wardrobe for Mrs MacRae in Letterfearn or a printing press for the *Stornoway Gazette* – but, as MacBrayne's 1912 Guide reported, she had: *"...excellent passenger accommodation and will be found extremely comfortable by those desirous of enjoying a week's sail (sleeping on board during night)"* She was sold for scrap in 1931.

**48.**     Some of the officers of the *SS Claymore*: Captain McAllister (2nd from left) with his chief engineer, chief steward and purser. A hand-coloured postcard *circa* 1903. At this time particularly, with passengers segregated, Cabin and 1st Class travellers had exclusive use of the Saloon and were more likely to meet these officers than those passengers travelling Steerage.

KYLE OF LOCHALSH, STATION AND PIER.
URQUHART DINGWALL SERIES

**49.** The paddle steamer ***Glencoe*** started life in 1846 as *Mary Jane* and was commissioned by James Matheson, owner of Lewis, for the conveyance of freight and passengers from Stornoway to the mainland. In 1857 she became part of David Hutcheson's fleet, and in 1875, after major alterations to her appearance, was renamed *Glencoe*. Her stations varied over the years but the Portree mail service was an important part of her duties. She made her final run from Skye in May, 1931, after an amazing eighty-five year career.

409. S.S. "Dunara Castle" at Kyle of Lochalsh

**50.** ***SS Dunara Castle:*** built in 1875 for Martin Orme, specifically for the conveyance of freight to the West Highlands. Some still remember her extended trips to the island of St. Kilda in the summer months prior to 1939. Throughout the year, *Dunara Castle* could be found *"plodding...from port to port, entering silent little lochs to discharge a cargo, or anchoring off some little townships to take on board sheep or cattle ..."* (Iain F. Anderson, **'Across Hebridean Seas'** 1937). Because of amalgamations and takeovers, she became part of MacBrayne's fleet in January, 1948, and was scrapped the same year.

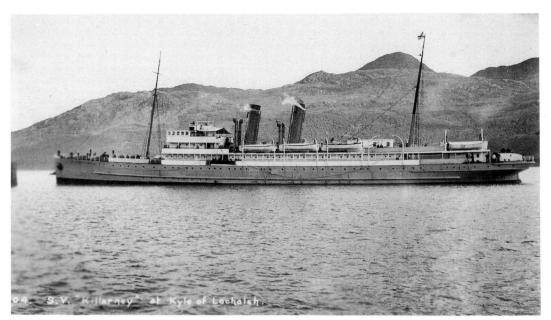

**51.** *SY Killarney* – a cruise ship sailing out of Liverpool to the Western Isles and the *"Scottish firths and fjords,"* as her owners Coast Line Ltd put it. She was always a welcome sight if anchored in a bay since her passengers were well-heeled and could be quite generous when buying souvenirs! *"Watching a cricket match between the locals and passengers,"* wrote the sender of this card, posted from Kyle in July 1933.

**52.** *SS Lochbroom* – formerly *City of London* – an iron ship built in 1871 for the route from London to Aberdeen, *Lochbroom* passed to MacBrayne's in 1931 and was the *first* to carry the name (the second *Lochbroom* was launched in 1948). She sailed from Glasgow with passengers and freight for west-coast ports, and was within a year of being scrapped when Duncan Macpherson produced this 1936 postcard.

**53.** The **SS Sheila**, launched 1904, flew MacBrayne's flag and carried cargo and passengers between Kyle and Stornoway for more than twenty years. Some of her trips were in horrendous conditions but praise was always reserved for her gallant crew who defied the Minch, summer and winter. Her luck finally ran out on 1 January 1927; while on passage from Stornoway to Kyle *via* Applecross she ran aground in Cuaig Bay and was a total loss. Fortunately, everyone on board was saved.

152. "LOCHNESS" At Kyle of Lochalsh

**54.** Built for MacBrayne's in 1929, **TSS Lochness** carried on where *Sheila* left off, but her appearance on the Mallaig-Kyle-Stornoway route had an interesting effect on the landscape of Kyle. Since *Lochness* fuelled at Kyle pier, a large and *very* prominent oil-storage tank had to be erected for her! Like pop band groupies, enthusiasts follow their favourite ships around various venues, but after her sale in the 1950s, fans of *Lochness* had to travel to Greece to find her under her new name: *Myrtidiotissa*.

**55.** **_TSMV Lochnevis_** was launched in 1934 for the all-important Mallaig to Portree mail service but World War II took her to other waters as _HMS Lochnevis_ – minelayer. The Mallaig-Portree service was curtailed in the 1940s when a boom was laid at Kylerhea to discourage enemy submarines. After the war _Lochnevis_ was stationed at various ports, Oban, Mallaig and Greenock included, and was withdrawn from service in the late 1960s. This postcard was posted in 1935 by Duncan Macpherson to his son Neil who was killed in the war.

**56.** An unusual visitor at Kyle Railway Pier: _TS King George V_ started life in the 1920s sailing between Greenock and Inveraray. In May, 1940, she was at Dunkirk but will be more familiar to the thousands who sailed on her after the war when she ran from Oban to Staffa and Iona. A private photograph generously loaned by Miss Flora and Miss Katherine Reid of Kyleakin.

**57.**    A *badly* faked postcard, *circa* 1949, published by Valentine's of Dundee who had previous form for this sort of deception. **TSMV Loch Seaforth** was launched in 1947 for the Stornoway mail service. The sender of this card was impressed with her in 1952 even if his facts were not quite accurate: *"This motor-ship goes from the railway at Kyle of Lochalsh across to the Isle of Lewis 80 miles away. It is about 500 tons,"* actually nearer 1,100 tons, *"and will take 200 or 300 people. It leaves Kyle about 2 in the afternoon and gets to Stornoway (which is a little town about as big as Ambleside) about 8 at night..."*

**58.**    The paddle steamer **Gael** at Kyle *circa* 1906. Built in 1867 for the Campbeltown & Glasgow Steam Packet Company, *Gael* was sold to the Great Western Railway Company in 1883 and for a period of eight years could be seen in the Channel, off Bristol and the Scilly Isles, and on a cross-channel service between Weymouth and Cherbourg. At the age of twenty-five (which was not too old for a Victorian paddle steamer) she was bought by David MacBrayne and returned to Scotland, initially to work the Oban-Gairloch route. She was scrapped in 1924.

**59.**    On board *Gael* at Kyle pier. Every Tuesday, Thursday and Saturday, the ship left Oban at 7 o'clock bound for Gairloch. If this was a Saturday jaunt these gentlemen had earned a rest: *Gael* had already visited Craignure, Lochaline, Salen, Tobermory, Eigg and Mallaig (all before noon), followed by Armadale, Glenelg and Balmacara. She was due in Kyle just before 2 p.m. with further calls at Kyleakin, Broadford and Portree. Gairloch was rarely reached by the scheduled time of 6.30 p.m.

**60.**    A view of **Kyle of Lochalsh** Railway Station from the deck of *Gael*. The full use of the name was important: the shortened form of 'Kyle' had been rejected by the Board of the Highland Railway Company from the outset.

**61.** In both world wars, Kyle of Lochalsh was a restricted area and generally out-of-bounds to all except residents and essential government personnel. This rare photograph, taken in 1918, shows men of the US Navy who were based in Kyle and involved with the unloading of supplies, shells, and the thousands of mines which were destined for Invergordon. It is said that Kyleakin had to be put out-of-bounds to the Americans because of their craving for souvenirs of Skye. They took things that were usually nailed down tight!

90. STATION HOTEL, KYLE OF LOCHALSH.

**62.** **The Station Hotel** *circa* 1914. A beautiful aspect for the residents but the interior lacked something much desired – light! Oil lamps lit the public rooms and guests were still carrying candles to light their way to bed in 1930! The directors of the LM & S Railway were not too pleased when they found out (it was an LMS hotel) and a generator was installed. Useful as this was, it had to be switched off at night because the noise kept everyone awake!

344.    Skye, Isle of Mist.

**63.** Our next destination: **'Skye, Isle of Mist'** as Duncan Macpherson captioned his 1930s postcard. Posted from Portree to Ramsgate in September, 1938, the writer has a few comments: *"This was the sort of view I had yesterday, but today, for a wonder, it is fine. The island is grand but the roads are ghastly. Makes Dumpton Road seem like a billiard table..."*

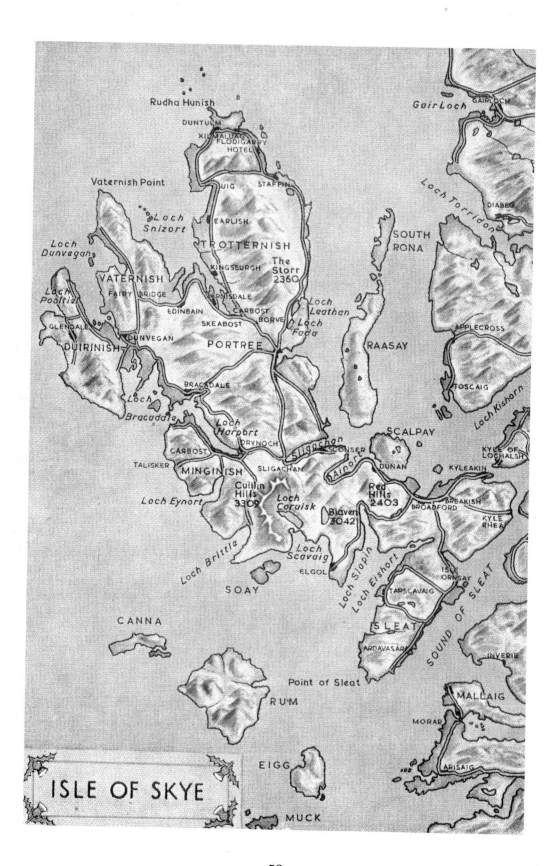

ISLE OF SKYE

# A CENTURY OF MOTORING

**S**ITTING ASTRIDE beasts of burden our distant ancestors trundled, somewhat uncomfortably, across dykes and ditches; then came that fateful day when one of them added a pair of newfangled wheels to a piece of wood and let the animal pull his contrivance. Later, from a donkey and cart, we moved to horse-drawn carriages and then to bicycles, and the dawn of personally-owned transport was finally upon us.

One hundred years ago, great-great grandfather had a go at steering a power-driven motor-cycle before entering the new century behind the wheel of an automobile. The reality of those years was put succinctly by André Maurois in **'King Edward and His Times'** (1933):

> *"It has been said that the coins of the Victorian Age should have been stamped, not with the Queen's effigy, but with a locomotive. The head of King Edward might perhaps have been replaced by a motor-car...but the eighteen-nineties were lived under the sign of the bicycle."*

Two years before the death of Queen Victoria, Edward, Prince of Wales experienced his first ride in a motor-car with Mr Scott-Montagu, M.P. who, as Lord Montagu of Beaulieu, was to become a Vice-President of the Royal Automobile Club with H.R.H. King Edward VII as Patron. The future monarch enjoyed the trip so much that he moved quickly to alter the coach-house at Buckingham Palace for the accommodation of his own motor-cars, albeit not until *after* his Coronation as mother would not have approved!

Far away from the Court of St. James, however, in the wilderness of the Highlands and Islands where incoming mail still had the words 'North Britain' or 'N.B.' as part of the address, things were a little different. Despite the existence of the Caledonian Motor Car and Cycle Company (1899-1906) in Aberdeen, the Mo-Car Syndicate in Glasgow, and the Hozier Engineering Company – builders of the 'Argyll' motor-car – there were no references to 'motor-cars', 'automobiles' or 'motor-cycles' within Ward Lock's 1905 **'Guide to the Highlands and Islands of Scotland'** apart from one. In the 'Useful Hints' section, sandwiched between 'Clothing' (*"...the traveller will rejoice if his ordinary clothing is warmer than he would have provided for the south of England"*) and 'The Sabbath' (*"...the day being much more rigorously observed in North Britain than in the country to the south of the Tweed"*), was the brief entry:

> *"A car or waggonette is the most common form of carriage for hire, and is known as a 'machine'."*

Unfortunately, the word 'car' was being used as a diminutive for a cart and not as a reference to the infant automobile: a car or waggonette was a horse-drawn vehicle in which the passengers sat behind the driver, on each side facing inwards. It was popularly called 'a machine' but one guide-book writer cautioned his readers on the hazards of travelling on it:

> *"...limited room for luggage, with no protection from the drippings of your neighbour's umbrella. The box-seat may sometimes prove a fearful joy to fastidious passengers if their driver indulge himself in chewing tobacco!"*

In 1905, trains or horse-drawn coaches provided the only reliable means of overland travel in the Highlands, but Ward Lock acknowledged the craze for bicycling by adding an appendix – 'For Cyclists' – to his guide that year. It gave a few details regarding the conveyance of bicycles on the rail and steamer routes, and hinted at the state of some of the more popular roads:

> *"From Callander to Oban the quality of the road is variable but the scenery is magnificent. The worst portion lies through Glen Lochy and should be avoided by taking the train from Tyndrum to Dalmally...from Fort William to Inverness there is a succession of ups and downs. As a rule the surface is excellent as far as Spean Bridge, less satisfactory to Drumnadrochit and very good beyond that...from Edinburgh to Perth and Inverness the route is through grandest scenery. There is a very difficult stretch of twenty miles between Bruar and Dalwhinnie, and some dangerous hills in the last twenty-five miles."*

Skye was particularly well-served by ships at this time and cyclists were advised to take a steamer to Portree and then " *'wheel it' through Skye"*. Writing in 1912, one guide-book compiler suggested that the cyclist made for Uig Inn on the first day *"...visiting Flora Macdonald's grave, Duntulum Castle and the eccentric Quiraing ..."* On the second day the advice was:

> *"...to go westwards to Dunvegan, with its castle, and down the coast to Loch Harport to Sligachan, where several days may be spent in exploring Loch Coruisk and the Coolins: then by the very hilly but magnificently wild road by Loch Ainort to Broadford, and so to Kyle Akin where there is a tempting little inn."*

The same writer made frequent mention of mail-carts, horse-drawn coaches and ponies, but had no advice for motorists wishing to visit the island.

Uig *circa* 1912.

Despite the fact that Motor Trials had been held in Glasgow in 1901 and reliability trials had taken place elsewhere under the auspices of the Scottish Automobile Club, a motor-car was still a novelty in 1905, something usually reserved for the nobility (their coach-men now called 'chauffeurs') or the more affluent members of Highland society. But whereas Ward Lock did not think it necessary to publish information that could be of use to 'automobilists', one of his advertisers did. The Pitlochry Hydro promised to provide *"Stabling for horses"* and cautiously added the words *"Cycle accommodation"* to their advertisement in 1905. In Nairn, the Imperial Golf Hotel compromised somewhat with *"Good Cycle Stables"*, but the Richmond Hotel in Tomintoul was fortunate in being *"Situated on the Driving route between Braemar...and Grantown"* and the management offered *"Motor House and Petrol"* for the use of their auto-owning guests. Then, within the space of five years, everything changed!

By 1908, publishers in Glasgow and Edinburgh were beginning to sit up and take notice of the motor-cars manoeuvring around their streets, frightening the horses, amusing the children but horrifying the old, and snippets of 'Motoring Information' crept into their guide-books, initially in the form of flimsy coloured pages hurriedly bound into the front of the volumes before the obligatory title-page. One such guide – with a paltry eight-page 'Pink Inset' from a total of over 450 pages – was the 1908 edition of Baddeley's **'Thorough Guide to Scotland'** published by Thomas Nelson of Edinburgh. In small print on the vivid puce-coloured pages, automobilists were advised of the state of certain roads:

*"...good all the way between Langholm and Hawick...dangerous into Galashiels...especially rough between Dalmally and Tyndrum..."*

Some hints were slightly more helpful, such as this reference to the road between Fort William and Mallaig:

*"There are no difficulties until after Kinloch Ailort, but thereafter it needs a low gear, a strong car and a strong driver to surmount the sharp, stony braes that abound farther on towards Mallaig. There are endless difficult and dangerous corners and turns, and it takes the best of driving and a car of not less than 15-20 h.p. to get through successfully."*

Thomas Telford's road to Mallaig still has its fair share of critics but there are plans for an upgrade in the future, or so it has been reported, regularly, over the years!

Justifiably praised for their beautifully illustrated guides to such places as Cairo, Constantinople, Paris and Rome, London-based publishers Adam and Charles Black also produced guide-books for destinations closer to home. In 1910, the fourteenth edition of **'Black's Shilling Guide to Scotland'** was released: a small hard-back volume packed with useful tips and wonderful advertisements for such products as medal-winning brandies from France or Ronuk sanitary polish – *"By Appointment to His Majesty the King"* – awarded a Gold Medal at the XVIIth International Congress of Medicine. Stuffed animals could be purchased from Peter Spicer & Sons of Inverness, *"Taxidermists to His Imperial Majesty the King of Spain"*, and Dr J. Collis Browne's 'Chlorodyne' provided *"The best remedy known for Coughs, Colds, Asthma...Toothache, Rheumatism, Gout...Palpitations, Hysteria, Cholera and...Diarrhoea."* What a fantastic cure-all that must have been!

But, once again, it was the hotel advertisers who were heralding the real changes. *"Accommodation for Motors free"* or *"our establishment holds Official Appointment of the Scottish Automobile Club"* now appeared frequently within the advertisements along with such words as *"Inspection Pit"* or *"Petrol and Oils stocked and repairs done."* Even on the island of North Uist, the manager of the Lochmaddy Hotel could boast of a *"Motor Car for hire"* in 1910, a distinct accomplishment in view of the statement from the Glasgow offices of David MacBrayne Ltd. just two years earlier:

*"The conditions which obtain in connection with the conveyance of motor-cars, and the landing of such at the various west coast ports and ferries, are such that it makes it quite impossible to give any estimate of the cost of their conveyance. In the first place, special arrangements would require to be made so far as piers are concerned, the weights of the cars &c., having also to be taken into account, while in most cases it would be necessary for arrangements to be made to suit the tide..."*

Black's 'Shilling Guide' of 1910 was one of the earliest publications to carry an advertisement placed by a Skye hotelier who also made reference to 'Motors'. The advert was placed by John Campbell of The Sligachan Hotel, but because all advertisements were pushed to the back of the guide and entered in alphabetical order, Campbell's effort appeared next to that for the Spiggie Hotel in Shetland and they had some really tempting offers to seduce the tourist:

*"Very suitable ground for Golf or Cricket...Croquet set provided. Good roads for Cycling...Seal Shooting near Fitful and Sumburgh Heads..."*

---

# ISLE OF SKYE.

Tourists wishing a quiet and pleasant holiday should come to **SKYE** and stay at **THE SLIGACHAN HOTEL,** under new management. Enlarged and Refurnished throughout.

Excursions arranged for **Loch Coruisk, Cuchullin Hills, Curang,** etc. The centre from which to do all Skye.

Carriages, Motors, Etc.

**Illustrated booklet on application, JOHN CAMPBELL.**

---

Sligachan Hotel advertisement from the 1910 edition of Black's 'Shilling Guide'.

Perhaps it is not surprising that, prior to the outbreak of the Great War, guide-books failed to recommend Skye to the motorist. Automobiles were few in number and the majority of owners still lived miles away in the larger towns and cities, but, more importantly, drivers had not yet exhausted their enthusiasm for speeding up and down *mainland* routes. Kyleakin, Broadford and Portree were well served by swift passenger steamers sailing from Oban, Mallaig, Kyle and Gairloch, and as far as

David MacBrayne was concerned automobiles were a thing of the future – if they ever caught on of course! The railway companies, however, had come to terms with the automobile, and in 1908 both the Highland Railway Company and the Great North of Scotland Railway Company were charging 7d per mile (minimum charge 7/6d) for a vehicle conveyed by passenger train between any station on their respective lines.

The only hotel on Skye to hold the 'Official Appointment' of the Scottish Automobile Club at this time was the Royal Hotel in Portree. To qualify for the honour the hotel had to provide certain services including accommodation for members' cars at a charge *"of not more than 1/- per 24 hours"*, making no charge for parking while the driver and passengers were *"merely partaking of meals or refreshments"*, and offering the car-owner the use of *"a hose pipe and water under pressure."* S.A.C. members staying at the Royal Hotel were charged 6/6d for bed, breakfast and attendance; once back on the mainland at Kyle, the nearest hotels with the prized 'Official Appointment' sign on their walls were the Station Hotel at Achnasheen, the Glenmoriston Hotel and the Invergarry Hotel.

In 1910, the year the king died, there were less than 46,000 private cars on the roads of Great Britain; in 1995, the number was in excess of 20 million. But regardless of the advantages that it might bring now, owning a motor-car was an expensive undertaking in Edwardian times, out of reach of ordinary folk and generally regarded as a leisure pursuit for the rich rather than a useful means of travelling for all. Many doctors, however, saw the advantages of car ownership, and their presence as Officers or Committee members with the national and regional automobile clubs was a testimony to their foresight and affluence. In fact it was the automobile clubs – with their highly influential members – that set the standards for future motorists in Great Britain and Ireland, and influence played a major role when it came to formulating motoring laws and practices.

Provincial motoring clubs affiliated to the Automobile Club (the 'Royal' prefix was granted in 1907) sprang up everywhere at the beginning of the century and committee members went to great lengths to secure the patronage of a titled president: Field-Marshal Roberts V.C. for the Berkshire Automobile Club; the Duke of Westminster for Cheshire A.C.; the Earl of Warwick for Essex County A.C. and the Earl of Derby for the Liverpool club. From the outset the stated objectives of the R.A.C. and its affiliated members were:

> *"The encouragement and development of the automobile movement; the provision for its members of a social club, and a centre of information and advice on matters pertaining to automobilism; and the advantage of its support in the protection and defence of their rights..."*

So it was particularly useful to have the support of His Majesty the King as Patron, H.R.H. the Prince of Wales as Vice-Patron, the Duke of Sutherland as President, and a worthy selection of Vice-Presidents including the Earls of Dudley and Onslow; Lords Stanley and Montagu of Beaulieu, Sir David Solomons, Bart., and Member of Parliament Mr C.D. Rose.

Similarly, the Motor Union of Great Britain and Ireland (M.U.) – a rival organisation to the R.A.C. – had Vice-Presidents who could also be relied upon *"to protect and extend the rights and privileges of motorists."* They included the Dukes of Beaufort, Rutland and Newcastle; the Earls of Aberdeen, Derby and Warwick, the Rt. Hon. Earl Roberts, K.G., K.P., V.C., and a variety of eminent knights, colonels and Members of Parliament. The M.U. also retained solicitors and honorary correspondents throughout the Kingdom. Their 1908 list names Messrs. John C. Brodie and Sons of Edinburgh as the sole appointed legal representative in Scotland, with Mr Macdonald of the Fife Arms Hotel in Braemar, Mr Buckmaster in Kinlochleven and Dr Gillies in Tain – along with others elsewhere – acting as local correspondents.

The Scottish Automobile Club was also well established at this time. The Rt. Hon. Sir J.H.A. Macdonald, K.C.B., P.C., LL.D. – Lord Justice-Clerk of Scotland – was President and he was ably assisted by a council of Vice-Presidents including the Dukes of Argyll and Sutherland; the Marquesses of Tweeddale, Bute and Breadalbane, Lords Saltoun, Napier and Etterick, Blythswood, Dunedin, and the Right Hon. Arthur James Balfour, M.P., P.C., F.R.S., D.C.L., LL.D., D.L. Names that came straight from the pages of Debrett's!

Thanks, particularly, to the lobbying-power of the many thousands of ardent cyclists, a 'Road Improvement Association' had been formed in 1886 with a view to obtaining for the public *"better, wider and more conveniently planned roads and footways."* No one should underestimate the tremendous good that those enthusiastic two-wheeled travellers achieved in pursuit of what, at that time, was just a pleasant hobby.

*"Propagandist activities by pedal cyclists,"* was how one writer described their deeds within the Association, but what propaganda! In 1890-91, £8.7 million was allocated to road maintenance; by 1903 this had risen to £14.6 million and with it came positive improvements in road quality. Over the next seven years, as the automobile trade expanded, the total amount spent on roads soared to £120 million.

Despite all the money, however, one major problem still dogged cyclist and automobilist alike – *dust!* When it wasn't raining it got everywhere. In the eyes if one forgot the goggles, in the hair if the hat was raised to a lady, or in the ears if the cap-flaps had not been tied down; certainly in the mouth if one took too deep a breath, but *always* it got up ones nose. True, it was more of a menace to the innocent bystander than it was to the automobile driver and his passengers but it still concerned the Council of the Road Improvement Association. Sitting on the council were members representing the Cyclists' Touring Club and the National Cyclists' Union; the Royal Automobile Club, the Motoring Union of G.B. and Ireland and many other interested parties, and they arranged trials to determine the most suitable type of road tar and a cost-effective method of spreading it mechanically. Regular tests were carried out on various public highways, particularly in the Home Counties, and as a result the Government and the local authorities were eventually able to overcome the dust problem. From Wade, Caulfield, Telford, Mitchell and McAdam, to the unnamed mechanical engineers and county surveyors from the early years of this century, a great debt of gratitude is owed for their pioneering efforts on behalf of all road-users past and present.

In the 1960s, one could drive up and down the M1 motorway at speeds in excess of 100 miles an hour; it was perfectly legal and, with less than 6 million vehicles, traffic was minimal. Given, then, a similar opportunity to speed along an empty Highland road sixty years earlier, many a dashing young automobilist would have been tempted too, but for them a speed limit *did* apply.

When steam-powered vehicles first appeared on our highways they were perceived to be a terrible danger to horses, children and the elderly, and a man with a red flag was required to walk in front of the offending machine and warn of its approach. This 1865 Locomotive Act – better known as the 'Red Flag' Act – was repealed in 1896, but the Motor Car Act of 1903 imposed other restrictions on the novice motorist. Generally speaking, early speed limits were fixed at between 10 and 14 miles per hour but in no circumstances was a driver permitted to exceed 20 miles per hour anywhere in Great Britain and Ireland. Section 8 of the Motor Car Act also gave discretionary powers to local authorities to fix limits below 10 m.p.h. if circumstances were such as to make it necessary, and the annual **'Automobile Handbook'** published the details in full. This is a typical example from 1908:

### ALFRISTON

*"Speed restricted to five miles per hour on so much of the road leading from Alfriston to Seaford as lies between a point opposite the north-eastern boundary of the garden attached to the cottages known as West Hill Cottages, Frog Firlie, and a point on the said road 90 ft. west of the point at which a footpath which leaves the said road opposite Tile Barn rejoins that road."*

Section 10 of the Motor Car Act allowed for warning notices and signposts to be erected by municipal and county authorities, and from 1904 onwards such signs began to proliferate by the road verges. The R.A.C. and the Motor Union were also erecting their own warning signs at this time, paying particular attention to schools, dangerous hills and concealed entrances. Then one more motoring organisation came onto the scene. Recognised today as the undisputed master and controller of route signs, the Automobile Association was formed in 1905, its aims being:

*"...the repression of furious and inconsiderate driving by its system of patrols; the provision of guides for motorists passing through the most important towns; and the naming of the villages by the erection of name-plates."*

One of a series of 'Road Sign' postcards published by the Automobile Association in the 1930s.

Sign-posting was important, but the chief concern of everyone at this time was speed and its effect on others. In 1905, a Leeds Corporation tramcar exceeded 18 m.p.h. during an official 'Speed Limit Inquiry', but in London – where else! – tram No. 159 beat that with a maximum speed of 21 miles an hour. On the Victoria

Embankment a year earlier, an official timekeeper had recorded hansom cabs travelling at up to 15.9 m.p.h., a railway omnibus doing 15.7 m.p.h. and a mail van exceeding 13 m.p.h., but in a special speed trial over a measured distance of 110 yards in Piccadilly, horse-drawn traps and broughams were still holding their own with speeds averaging 13.9 miles an hour. Then along came a humble, presumably very fit cyclist who left them all gasping at his 15.85 miles an hour!

With some vehicles now capable of reaching speeds in excess of 60 miles an hour, the legal limit may have appeared unreasonable in view of the speed achieved by horses and bicycles. Driving a £1,000, 50 h.p. four-cylinder Talbot automobile in 1910, the Earl of Aberdeen's chauffeur would certainly not have looked too kindly on the cyclist who dared to attempt to overtake him in a 10 m.p.h. zone, but at this juncture I will pause and declare a personal interest in a 'speeding matter' before continuing the story of His Lordship's driver.

Between 1962 and 1968, this writer lived and worked in central London and remembers only too well the activities of the police as they supervised the area around Victoria Street and Vauxhall Bridge Road during the evening rush-hour. Rush 'hour' usually started at 4.30 p.m. and a driver would think himself fortunate if the traffic between Victoria Station and Vauxhall Bridge was back to normal before 6.30 p.m.

Monday to Friday, January to December, at half past four precisely, officers from Rochester Row police station would position themselves along the entire length of the aforementioned route, and at some undetermined time after that – but apparently at the whim of one all-seeing constable at the Victoria end of Vauxhall Bridge Road – long white silken arm-bands would appear from secret inner pockets, and as converging cars and crowded buses battled for the last remaining space on Vauxhall Bridge Road, the constables donned their arm-bands and the traffic lights went out! Panic was momentary. Traffic was virtually at a standstill anyway and the police were quick to move into the centre of the road. Jumping the red light was no longer a driver's option now, but ignoring the raised arm of the constable brought instant and noisy retribution when his black-gloved hand struck the flimsy roof of your car as you drove by. You didn't stop, you weren't really expected to, but you knew that the officer had intended you to be the *first* car in the new queue and not the last to get by him!

Further along Vauxhall Bridge Road, other officers would be stood on traffic islands, monitoring the traffic flow, looking for out-dated or missing tax discs or reporting motor-cyclists who overtook on the wrong side of a 'Keep Left' bollard. But at six o'clock those same officers took on a quite different role. With frantic arm movements and occasional shouts of encouragement they attempted to speed up the now diminishing traffic queues, urging tardy or law-abiding motorists to catch up with the car ahead. The 30 m.p.h. speed limit was of no concern to the officers; the quicker the motorist was clear of Victoria and had crossed over Vauxhall Bridge into a different police division, the sooner they could go for their meal-break or sneak a coffee in the kitchen of the local Aberdeen Angus Steak House. Your speedometer might be showing 34...38...46 m.p.h., but the officers were in charge and you wanted to get home just as much as they wanted you to. One wonders now if any of those young officers were aware of the comments made by a certain Mr Filson Young:

> *"The object of the law, with which we are all in sympathy, is the protection of the public. Yet how do the police as a body act in applying it? Do they use every effort to discourage excessive speed on the part of the individual motorist? On the contrary, they use every subterfuge to tempt and entrap him into excessive speed. Their object is not to prevent him from breaking the law, but to induce him to do*

*so; hence their traps on empty and tempting stretches of road, where speed is not dangerous at all. If the police were seen about the roads, no motorist would dare drive at an excessive speed; but when they hide behind hedges, they are merely acting as spies and not as constables of the public safety. This 'hedging and ditching' policy, apart from its injustice, is a discredit to, and a blot on, the traditions of the police."*

Filson Young may have been caught speeding some time in his life – it matters not really – but since his remarks appeared in the revised 1907 edition of **'The Complete Motorist'** (first published in September 1904), this writer can honestly say that, to the best of his knowledge, Mr Young did not ignore *his* hand signals in Victoria in the 1960s or exceed the 30 m.p.h. speed limit in Vauxhall Bridge Road at his insistence!

The Earl of Aberdeen was just about to be overtaken by an enthusiastic cyclist when we left him and His Lordship's chauffeur was not amused; he responded accordingly, accelerated past the hapless two-wheeler, and continued at speed along an empty country road until he fell foul of the local constabulary.

To prove that an automobilist was speeding was quite subjective in the early 1900s. The favoured method of detection was for two constables to time a vehicle between marker posts – or at the drop of a handkerchief – using a stop-watch. Allegations that the officer's watch was running fast, or that he pressed its button or waved his handkerchief a little too late, were not uncommon, but the motorist might actually argue with the officers without even knowing what his speed had been. As Young recorded, a speedometer was just one of the optional fittings *"which the enthusiast may have upon his dashboard – most of them very costly and of doubtful utility."* Young also maintained that a good carriage clock was *"a necessity"* but *"on the whole I do not advise the ordinary motorist to have a speed recorder."* Acknowledging this problem, our Edwardian legislators generously agreed that a driving licence should only be endorsed when a driver committed his third speeding offence; fortunate, indeed, the chauffeur whose employer was also a titled vice-president of the Motor Union of G.B. and Ireland!

As a footnote to this diversion, the ultimate accolade for speeding must go to a Frenchman by the name of Camille Jenatzy who, in April 1899, became the first man in history to drive an automobile on a public highway at a speed in excess of a mile a minute. He achieved 65.79 m.p.h. in an *electric* car, only to see his record broken in 1902 when a *steam* car sped by at 75 miles an hour! Both steam and electric motors played an important and distinguished role in the early history of vehicular transport – a steam-driven coach had actually run between Glasgow and Paisley in 1834 and the first vehicle on Skye is said to have been a steam car – but steam and electric lost out to petroleum and we may all die regretting it.

Many of our current motoring laws date from the first decade of this century, yet those Edwardian laws had an antecedent in the Highways Act of 1835 when drivers were warned that they should not leave their carriages on the highway so as to cause an obstruction or that they should keep to the left or near-side of the road. Penalties were particularly severe, and fines of up to £10 were imposed on offending owners (their servants were only fined to a £5 maximum) with jail terms of up to six weeks with hard labour for non-payment of fines.

The railway system was still in its infancy in the 1830s but horse-drawn coaches had been travelling the length and breadth of the Kingdom for many decades and good speeds were regularly achieved on certain routes. The London-bound 'Birmingham

Independent Tally-Ho' could cover the 109 miles at an average speed of 14.25 m.p.h. while the express coach from Shrewsbury to London – the 'Shrewsbury Wonder' – averaged 17 m.p.h. over 158 miles; the stopping version took an extra five hours to cover the same route. Doubtless all coachmen were aware of the new offence of *"driving a carriage furiously so as to endanger the life or limb of any passenger"*, but just in case anyone should think this precept is archaic and long-forgotten, be warned! In 1994, a horse trader in Yorkshire was fined £100 for *"wanton and furious driving"* of his rig when he overtook a police car, went downhill at over 25 m.p.h., then crossed the central white-line as his horse and cart shot over the brow of the next hill!

Comparing speed and quality of coaches south of the Border with those in the Highlands is unfair in view of the differing terrains, but the northern network was certainly extensive as a 'Time Bill' for 1858 reveals. With a map showing the routes of the Glencoe and Glenorchy coaches, and their links with steamers and other coaches, it advertised:

*"Daily, direct and rapid coach and steamer conveyance through the Highlands by Glencoe and Glenorchy Coaches in connection with the coaches 'Marquis of Breadalbane' to Loch-Tay, Taymouth and Aberfeldy, and new coaches between Oban and Tarbet by Inveraray...from Glasgow to Fort-William, Inverness or Aberfeldy...from Oban via Inveraray to Loch-Lomond every lawful day at 8.30 a.m....from Fort-William to Glasgow every lawful day at 6.00 a.m....between Dunkeld and Inverness...between Callander and Loch-Katrine...between Loch-Katrine and Loch-Lomond, where a New Road has been made..."*

An original Time Bill of 1858.

While no precise journey times were given, apart from the intended hour of departure, passengers would have expected some delays and accepted them stoically. The operators placed more emphasis on the state of their coaches rather than on the ability of the driver to keep to a time-table:

*"These coaches are constructed on a principle embracing all recent improvements, and built expressly for these lines – the Horses strong, and the whole working arrangements perfected, so as to secure the comfort and safety of Tourists."*

Just two fares are shown on the Time Bill: 22/- for the Tarbet to Oban journey and 22/6d for the Glasgow to Fort William trip. The latter price included fees of 1/- for the driver and 1/6d for the guard; 'front' or 'inside' seats cost an extra five shillings on either route. In 1889, the coach on the Kingussie to Fort William route took six and three-quarter hours to cover the fifty-one miles at an average of just under 8 miles an hour; if, however, a passenger wanted to travel the extra 40 miles to Arisaig in order to catch one of Mr MacBrayne's swift steamers, that took a further eight hours!

Old Highland tracks, originally made by an ancient race of people, had become regularly-used footpaths or drove roads within a very short space of time. The military cart tracks of the eighteenth century were soon turned into single-track roads for civilian use, but in the last few years of the nineteenth century pedestrians were forced on to the grassy verges as cycles and automobiles competed for space alongside the horse. Later, these same roads were widened to allow vehicles to pass without having to stop. Then dual carriageways were introduced so that drivers could overtake without hindering oncoming traffic and eventually the motorway concept took over, although, fortunately, not on the island of Skye. The result? An extra dimension for us all; the ability to move across the surface of the earth faster than any previous generation!

In 1995, Scotland celebrated a century of motoring and Skye was finally linked to the mainland by a bridge, but within the last sixty years many of the earlier roads have been bypassed or altered almost beyond recognition.

Of the routes to Kyle of Lochalsh, the most obvious changes include the A890 by Loch Carron, the 'new' road from Balmacara (avoiding Erbusaig), the bridge over Loch Long and so *many* more. On Skye, meanwhile, roads were also being altered or improved, and in May, 1939, the AA issued the following advice to their members:

*"Reconstruction is taking place from Kyleakin to 4 miles beyond Broadford, then narrow and fair to good, with poor stretches round by Sligachan, Dunvegan to Duntulum, then reconstruction work to Staffin (3 miles). The remainder to Portree is poor. South of Portree is good for 3 miles then reconstruction work to Sligachan (6.5 miles). Side roads leading to the coast are generally very narrow with poor loose surface."*

Since 1939, the roads of Skye have been upgraded, but as many of the illustrations in the second part of this book were taken before then, the photographs show very few vehicles. Today, however, heavy lorries move regularly between Uig and Kyleakin. Couple these with the summer visitor traffic and the roads can be exceptionally busy. Sheep will *always* slow the traveller in a hurry (*illus.* **81**) but mishaps like the one on the Luib road many years ago (*illus.* **83**) are fairly rare so relax and enjoy the rest of the nostalgic tour!

# KYLEAKIN TO SLIGACHAN WITH DIVERSIONS

**64.** The lighthouse on *Eilean Ban* – a photograph taken in 1907 when the light celebrated its fiftieth birthday. *"The light-keepers' children were ferried by boat to Kyleakin school,"* commented Mary Macpherson in **'Memories of Kyleakin'** published in 1950. Born in 1882, Mary recalled that in her day *"…there were eight or nine children coming from the lighthouse. The school was left open at the dinner hour to have their lunch, which they carried."* The island now acts as a support for the Skye Bridge.

**65.** A hand-coloured postcard produced in Saxony, *circa* 1903, for Donald Macpherson to sell exclusively from Kyleakin post office.

A HIGHLAND CARGO, KYLEAKIN, SKYE.

**66.** For centuries, Skye cattle fairs and sales attracted mainland buyers; it was the responsibility of the drovers, however, to get the beasts off the island at the end of the day. At Kylerhea the animals swam across, but at Kyleakin, **'H.R. No.2'** – a Highland Railway barge – was used for the purpose and the beasts were landed at a point *behind* the Lochalsh Hotel.

LANDING AT KYLEAKIN, SKYE.

B.1390.

**67.** A still day in the 1940s: barely a ripple on the water, and the all-wood car-ferry *Moil* is at the pier while travellers from the passenger-ferry board the Portree bus or stroll towards the village after their journey from Kyle.

6900 Kyleakin Pier and the Kyle of Lochalsh, Isle of Skye.

**68.** A panoramic view across Kyleakin harbour in the 1930s. An excellent place from which to see Skye Bridge. The little climb will reward photographers and sightseers alike.

The Pier, Kyleakin, Skye

**69.**     The centre of activity and a life-line to the outside world – **Kyleakin Pier** (now long gone although the stumps are still visible) as it looked *circa* 1912. *"The village is a pleasant resting-place for tourist and artist, commanding some of the finest landscapes in the Western Highlands,"* according to MacBrayne's **'Summer Tours in the Western Highlands and Islands of Scotland'** 1912 edition.

6911 Kyleakin, Isle of Skye.

**70.**     With the increase in ferry-traffic in the 1960s, the grassy area between bay and road was eventually turned into a parking area so that the queue – in this part of the village at least – could be channelled away from the main road. This is how it looked in the 1930s.

**71.** Contrasting postcards: the **Marine** and **Heathmount** Hotels in the late 1950s…

**72.** …with the 'new & improved' version of the **Marine** Hotel (now the Youth Hostel) on a postcard from the 1960s.

**73.** The exterior of the **Kings Arms Hotel** on a hand-coloured card posted from Kyleakin to Glasgow in August, 1909, with a message that must have been written so many times during the past one hundred years: *"Having a fine time in Skye."*

**74.** Postcards of hotel interiors are fairly unusual but the proprietor of the **Kings Arms** was obviously proud of his dining room. A black and white postcard written by a guest – *"Staying here for three nights, touring Skye ..."* – in August, 1958, almost half-a-century after the previous picture.

**75.** *"Broadford is a post town, containing a lime kiln, an inn, and perhaps three dozen houses in all. It is a place of great importance. If Portree is the London of Skye, Broadford is its Manchester."* (Alexander Smith, **'A Summer in Skye'** 1865). Not quite in the Manchester mould 130 years on, Broadford still has so much to offer modern-day travellers. If they would only slow down on entering the village – *who mentioned the radar trap?* – and stop for an hour or two!

**76.** A 1950s art-card of **Broadford** produced by Valentine's of Dundee using watercolours by Edward H. Thompson.

**77.** **The James Ross Memorial Fountain** now languishes at the bottom of the public car park below Sutherlands garage and emporium. With water in mind, a footnote in **'In the Hebrides'** (C.F. Gordon Cummings, 1883) mentions the schoolmaster in Broadford who registered the local rainfall in the 1870s. In one year he measured 98 inches but was particularly proud of 1877 when he was able to record rain on two hundred days!

**78.** Rural sub post offices in Skye have always played an important part in the life of the community. The **Torrin** office (under the control of the main office in Broadford) opened in 1898 and, like Elgol below, was served either by runner or, as the century drew to a close, by horse post; bicycles came later and in 1908 The Braes office was the first to switch to this form of delivery.

**79.**  *"We drove through varied and superb scenery to a little village called Elgol...a tiny hamlet of about a score of crofts, fishing huts and a post-office ..."* (Dr Walter Mursell **'Isles of Sunset'** 1931). The sub office of **Elgol** (also under Broadford) opened in 1880. Both views of Torrin and Elgol are from the 1930s.

LANDING AT LOCH SCAVAIG FOR LOCH CORUISK
ISLE OF SKYE

**80.** Passengers embark for their trip from Loch Scavaig to Loch Coruisk. A postcard produced anonymously some thirty years ago. It must have been a very hot day: the two men at the back of the queue have knotted handkerchiefs on their heads! The boat now operating on this route (toilet included) is licensed and insured for twelve passengers. Twenty-four potential sailors (*not* counting the crew) can be seen in this picture.

169. SLIGICHAN ROAD.
BROADFORD SKYE.

**81.** From loch to land: the Portree-bound bus gives way to a flock of sheep on the road out of Broadford. A photograph taken by Duncan Macpherson and published as a postcard prior to May, 1932, the year this example was posted.

6871 A Township of Skye.

**82.** Still that strong mixture of 'ancient and modern' in this view of Luib – **'A Township of Skye'** – in the 1930s.

**83.** An 'incident' on the Luib road in the 1950s and Duncan Macpherson just happened to be passing – with his camera, of course. A little boy pokes at the fuel tank while his wiser, older companion watches the photographer. Perhaps they still remember that day!

**84.**     The grandeur of the famed **Coolins** of which so much has been written that any further comment would be superfluous...

373. Glamaig, from Sligachan

**85.**     ...and the extraordinary 2537 feet of **Glamaig** from Sligachan.

In Skye - "The Far Coolins are calling me away"

**86.** Stout boots, thick socks, rucksack and rope: the lady is ready for her day on the hills in the 1930s.

**87.   Marsco** (over 2400 ft) towering over the hotel at Sligachan: *"The inn, though small, is comfortable enough and affords shelter to a a wondrously varied multitude of tourists and travellers, members of the Alpine club, distinguished artists, statesmen, ecclesiastics, botanists, geologists, yachting parties...drovers, excisemen, down to that class of tourist who "does" Skye as a sort of unpleasant duty ..."* Comments by Mrs C. Gordon Cumming in her book **'In the Hebrides'** published 1883.

Sligachan Hotel, Isle of Skye.

**88.**   A picture that puts **Sligachan Hotel** in splendid isolation! *"In the memorable far-off days,"* wrote Thomas Nicol in 1935 in **'Through Bracken and Heather'**, *"this palatial abode consisted only of two rooms, and the present hall now occupies the site. There were no trees in front at that time, so that they must have been of a more recent addition."*

**89.**   An **Octogenarian spinner** – a photograph taken in the vicinity of what is now Viewfield Road, Portree, *circa* 1904.

**90.**   The street with 'most of the shops': **Wentworth Street** as it was in the early 1950s when traffic moved both ways. For those who have been away from Skye for any length of time, a one-way traffic scheme is now in operation and the street cannot now be accessed from Somerled Square.

**91.** Down to the pier: **Quay Brae** *circa* 1903. The present Post Office has now been relocated on the brow; the Royal Bank of Scotland operates from the building on the right of the picture.

THE HARBOUR, PORTREE

**92.** A view of the harbour *circa* 1918, and the tall masts of a sailing ship reach up from the quay side.

14758. PORTREE, THE PIER, ISLE OF SKYE – JUDGES LTD

**93.** A fine study of the pier at Portree: a postcard published by Judges of Hastings in the 1930s. Fortunately, many of their original celluloid and glass negatives of Scotland are preserved at their premises in St. Leonards-on-Sea, East Sussex.

**94.** The taker of the previous picture has now moved down to the pier for a better view of MacBrayne's paddle steamer *Fusilier*: built in 1888, sold in the mid-thirties and finally scrapped in 1939.

6888 Portree from the Harbour, Isle of Skye.

**95.** *"Portree is the capital of Skye, but it is not an exhilarating spot at which to land. It gives no promise whatever of the glories beyond…matters are not improved by the habit of the residenters about the harbour of dumping their household refuse into it."* (Dr Walter Mursell's remarks after landing in June, 1930). The Portree Harbour Redevelopment Group has plans that could change all that!

753/92

HE LODGE, PORTREE

**96.** Formerly a Victorian lodge for the use of Lady MacDonald, this is now the award-winning **Cuillin Hills Hotel.** With its 4 Crowns – Highly Commended category from the Scottish Tourist Board, and a Red Rosette from the AA for the quality of the food, this is an ideal spot from which to contemplate Portree Bay while sampling the hospitality. If a sea-mist obscures your view, have a look at the beautiful framed photographs of old Skye instead!

Post Office

STAFFIN from Garrafad

**97.** Away, now, from the bustle of Portree and *en route* to Uig: a distant view of **Staffin** from Garafad *circa* 1910.

KILT ROCK, STAFFIN, SKYE

**98.** The magnificence of **Kilt Rock** with a rock formation that will be familiar to all who have visited Fingal's Cave on Staffa. Road signs will guide the motorist to the car-park after which it is but a short walk to the viewing places.

MIST OVER THE QUIRAING, STAFFIN, SKYE. 215006.

**99.** The road through **Staffin** as it was *circa* 1952. Certainly fewer houses then.

THE WINDING ROAD THROUGH THE QUIRANG, ISLE OF SKYE. 6877

**100.** A formidable task for the driver of the 1920s vehicle as it grinds its way up and through the **Quiraing.**

Flodigarry Cottage, Skye. Home of Flora Macdonald

**101.** A late 1920s postcard of **Flodigarry Cottage,** a building standing on the site of what was Flora MacDonald's married home after 1751. Completely renovated, this building is now an annexe of Flodigarry Hotel and provides comfortable accommodation in delightful surroundings.

6914 Flodigarry Hotel, Isle of Skye

**102.** Built in 1895 as a private residence for Major R. Livingston MacDonald, a descendant of Flora, **Flodigarry** was converted into an hotel after his death in 1926. It still retains much of the charm and quaintness of a Victorian residence (bells that when pushed still bring the management or staff to your side!) and the food and service is of the very highest order. One writer, however, upon visiting the hotel shortly after it opened, thought it a pity that it had not been furnished in a more simple fashion and more in keeping with the time of Flora MacDonald!

**103.** The ruin of **Duntulum Castle** as it was sixty-five years ago. The forces of Nature have taken their inevitable toll, especially over the past decade, and even less of the building now remains.

**104.** Between Duntulum and Uig lies Kilmuir Churchyard (resting place of Flora MacDonald) and the Skye Museum of Island Life with its collection of thatched buildings similar to these which were actually in Portree. *"One of these little cottages I entered in the neighbourhood of the Quiraing…a tiny place built of rough-hewn stones and roofed with thatch; within was a stone floor, a modern grate…an odd chair or two, a dresser of dishes, a small table below the window…fowls, dogs and children moved freely about the floor…the walls were roughly papered with newspapers …"* (Dr Walter Mursell on visiting Skye in 1930).

**105.** The hairpin bend on the approach to Uig: the road surface has been *much* improved since this picture was taken in the 1930s! In days past, the crofters of Uig took their peat from beds further up the road then transported it to this bend. The peat was then put into sacks or baskets and lowered by a rope attached to a pole placed here for that specific purpose.

**106.** Edward VII's Coronation – postponed from June, 1902, because of an operation to remove the royal appendix – took place on 9 August; on 1 September, His Majesty and Queen Alexandra stopped off at Uig while on passage to Stornoway. The pier was already eight years old but the King 'officially' opened it during his day-trip. Reputedly 1,300 feet in length at the time – and who would doubt it! – it dominates the scene on this contemporary postcard issued *circa* 1903.

John Martin Hospital,                    Uig, Isle of Skye

**107.** The **John Martin Hospital** (built 1905) at Uig *circa* 1920, the site of Uig Youth Hostel today.

John Martin Hospital
Uig Skye
Feb 26 1930

Pay to Nurse Tulloch the sum of
£16. 5/- being Ge salary from Nov 28th
until Feb 28th at the rate of £65 per a.

M. Tulloch

Salary to 28th February, 1930.          £16:  5: –
N.H.I 13 weeks   @ 6d.                    –:  6:  6
                                         £15: 18: 6

Received payment with thanks
26. 2. 30.                                28. 2. 30

John Martin Hospital
Uig Skye
Feb 26th 1930.

Pay to Mary Macdonald maid the
sum of six pound ten Shillings
£ 6. 10/- being wages due from Nov 30th
until Feb. 28th at the rate of £26 per a.

                    Wages.        £6: 10: –
          N.H.I. 13 wks @ 6d.     –:  6:  6
M. Tulloch                        £ 6:  3:  6

                              Mary Donald.
                              Received with thanks

26. 2. 30.

**108.**    Surprised at the ephemeral things that survive flood, fire and wars? In 1995, these John Martin Hospital Trust receipts turned up at an auction in Cheshire along with a pile of other Skye-related documents. Nurse Tulloch's 1930 salary of £65 had risen to £80 by 1934 while maid Mary MacDonald 'got by' on £26 a year.

**109.** Yet one more former Victorian hunting lodge. A view of **Skeabost House** taken *circa* 1950 the year it was converted for use as an hotel. *"Good beds, good hot water supply with hand basins in bedrooms, good food from Home Farm ..."* were some of the remarks appearing in a contemporary advertisement then, and the crowds on Sunday highlight the excellence of the buffet lunch nearly half-a-century later!

**110.** Not all the grand Skye houses still stand; **Waternish House,** once owned by Victorian naturalist Captain Allan Macdonald, is now a ruin.

**111.** *"The night has passed. With the early morning our ship quietly glides down Loch Dunvegan, and as we glance from our cabin port-hole, the majestic picture of Dunvegan Castle slips by ..."* (Iain F. Anderson, **'Across Hebridean Seas'** 1937) An art card showing the SS *Hebrides* at Dunvegan Pier.

**112.** *"During the season, the castle is open to visitors on two afternoons a week, Tuesday and Thursday, from 2 to 5. The admission fee of one shilling is devoted to Dunvegan charities."* That was in the thirties; now it is a seven-day-a-week venture (March to October), and the admission charge has gone up somewhat! Seat of the Chiefs of MacLeod for nearly eight centuries, MacLeod clan treasures and fine Georgian furniture rub shoulders with the commercial activities that are so necessary if such buildings are to survive.

**113.** A Skye postman (Donald Murchison) at work in the 1920s. Admittedly, Donald's route did not include Dunvegan but he serves as an introduction to the next illustration!

**114.** An envelope – sadly, lacking its contents now – posted in Preston, Lancashire, on Monday 5 October, 1885, to John Hargreaves at Dunvegan Castle. On the back of the envelope are two 'Receiving' marks: the first records the arrival of the envelope at Portree on Tuesday 6 October, the second mark was made at Dunvegan prior to delivery to the castle on the Wednesday morning. A fast service indeed.

DUNVEGAN AND THE CUILLINS, SKYE.

B.1430.

**115.**   No sign of life and just a solitary car in this 1950s postcard view of **Dunvegan Village** produced by Valentine's of Dundee.

THE AIGEACH AND NEIST POINT LIGHTHOUSE, ISLE OF SKYE.

6988.

**116.**   As far west as one can go on Skye: **Neist Point** lighthouse, lighted in 1909 but as with many Scottish lights fully automatic now. Should you fancy a holiday out here, one of the keepers' cottages has rooms and a communal double kitchen for overnight use, while two other cottages provide self-catering accommodation for longer periods.

**117.** *"...through lovely Bracadale...we come to Struan, a veritable artist's paradise. Here I have seen the most beautiful carpet of primroses shining green and gold in the sun. Also here I have tasted the finest omelets outside Brittany, but I leave you to find for yourself the unassuming house in Struan of the sweet lady who makes them."* (Catriona MacIver, **'On Foot in the Western Isles'** 1933). The Wall's sign has now been replaced by one for a Mace shop while next door, Macleod's Tables restaurant provides food and a good pot of coffee at a *very* good price!

**118.  Spinning Wool in Skye:** a fine study from the studio of George Washington Wilson, published as a hand-coloured postcard at the turn of the century. Wilson died in 1893 and never saw postcards of his works: the first British *picture* postcard was only approved for use in 1895. Posted from Kingussie to Hove, Sussex, in 1907, the female sender has taken up a new sport: *"I am learning to play Golf; it is much better than tennis..."*

**119.**    Another Victorian photograph from the G.W. Wilson studio, published as an Edwardian postcard *circa* 1904. A variant of this **Skye Crofter picture** exists showing the man leaning on his *cas chrom* (foot plough).

Duisdale Hotel, Isle Ornsay, Isle of Skye.

**120.** A 1930s postcard showing **Duisdale Hotel** with its thick covering of ivy (now removed). Another Victorian lodge which survived the lean periods after the Great War, when taxes and social changes reduced the status of owners, it flourishes now as a comfortable hotel.

**121.** Perhaps it may be unfair to use the word, but *'pretty'* is the initial reaction of those who visit **Isle Ornsay** for the first time. The hotel, Eilean Iarmain, (not visible in this picture) is the chief attraction, but the small white building on the left of this picture has been converted into a gallery – *An talla Dearg taisbeanadh Gallery* – and is usually open from July until the end of the season.

Tarskavaig, Isle of Skye.

**122.** Back on the road to Armadale after Isleornsay, a signpost points to **Tarskavaig**. This is not a *detour* for drivers hurrying to catch the ferry (and those of a nervous disposition would be well advised to steer clear of it) but the road will have some unexpected little rewards for those who venture along its entire length.

ARMADALE CASTLE, SKYE

**123.** Completed in 1815, **Armadale Castle** fell on hard times and was virtually derelict fifty years ago. It is perhaps better known as the *Clan Donald Visitor Centre* today, with the old Victorian stables and carriage area (to the right of the main entrance in this early 1900s postcard housing the gift shop and restaurant.

Armadale Pier, Skye

**124.**   Our route back to the mainland (Mallaig) takes us down to **Armadale Pier**. In this 1920s postcard, the passengers have just disembarked from the *SS Claymore (illus.* **47**) and paid the 2d Landing Charge demanded by the man at the pier on behalf of Lord MacDonald whose land they were now on. If you have time to spare before the ferry sails, pop into the Ragamuffin shop and treat yourself to a sweater or jacket!

**125.**   Farewell to Skye! To accompany this picture of Armadale pier, taken by Duncan Macpherson in the thirties, some thoughts from author and enthusiastic sailor Iain Anderson as he sailed around Skye aboard the *SS Hebrides* in 1932: *"The simplicity of the Isles life particularly close to the mainland is disappearing and modern conditions with their resultant haste are gradually taking its place. The single wire of a crude aerial is today a not uncommon sight beside the cottage on the wind-swept moorlands. The lone cottager today looks through his wireless window into the whirling vortex of modernity."* Then came television: video receivers: satellite dishes: Skye Bridge and...well, what does the next century have in store for the crofters of Skye?

# Over the sea to Skye

## BY MACBRAYNE ....

MacBrayne ships and coaches provide smooth, luxurious travel around this supreme beauty spot. There is a daily steamer service to Skye from Mallaig and Kyle of Lochalsh connecting with the rail services from Glasgow. The sail from Mallaig to Portree, via the sound of Sleat, should on no account be missed. There is also a daily bus service between Ardvasar, Armadale and Kyleakin. Motor coach tours operate from Armadale and Ardvasar to Portree, Dunvegan Castle, Sligachan, Staffin and Uig, Kyleakin, etc.

*For further particulars of tours, times and fares etc. apply to:—*

## DAVID MACBRAYNE LTD.

Garage-Office: Ardvasar　°○°　Steam Packet Office: Portree
Isle of Skye

# BOOKS BY THE SAME AUTHOR:

Last Greetings from St. Kilda............................................... 1989
(several reprints – latest 1995)

The Summer of '89............................................................... 1990

The Western Isles – A Postcard Tour 1. Barra to North Uist.......... 1992

Shipwrecked on Vatersay!................................................. 1992

A Voyage to St. Kilda....................................................... 1993

The Western Isles – A Postcard Tour 2. Harris and Lewis.............. 1993

Iona and Staffa via Oban ('Nostalgic Album Views' Series).............. 1994

Over to Skye...Before the Bridge! ('Nostalgic Album Views' Series)... 1995

# JOINT AUTHOR:

Skye: A Postcard Tour (Bob Charnley & Roger Miket)..................... 1991
(reprinted 1995)